Life in Medieval Europe

The Church in Medieval Europe

Danielle Watson

Cavendish Square
New York

A portion of the material in this book has been derived from *Everyday Life in Medieval Europe* by Kathryn Hinds.

Published in 2017 by Cavendish Square Publishing, LLC
243 5th Avenue, Suite 136, New York, NY 10016

First Edition

CPSIA Compliance Information: Batch #CS16CSQ

All websites were available and accurate when this book was sent to press.

Library of Congress Cataloging-in-Publication Data

Names: Watson, Danielle, 1978- author.
Title: The church in medieval Europe / Danielle Watson.
Description: New York : Cavendish Square Publishing, 2016. | Series: Life in medieval Europe | Includes bibliographical references and index. |
Description based on print version record and CIP data provided by publisher; resource not viewed.
Identifiers: LCCN 2016001610 (print) | LCCN 2016000269 (ebook) |
ISBN 9781502618856 (ebook) | ISBN 9781502618849 (library bound)
Subjects: LCSH: Europe--Church history--600-1500.
Classification: LCC BR750 (print) | LCC BR750 .W37 2016 (ebook) |
DDC 274/.03--dc23
LC record available at http://lccn.loc.gov/2016001610

Editorial Director: David McNamara
Editor: Kelly Spence
Copy Editor: Nathan Heidelberger
Art Director: Jeffrey Talbot
Designer: Joseph Macri
Production Assistant: Karol Szymczuk
Photo Research: J8 Media

The photographs in this book are used by permission and through the courtesy of: Hans Musil/File:Canterbury Cathedral - Portal Nave Cross-spire.jpeg/Wikimedia Commons, cover; Ron Ellis/Shutterstock.com, 4; APIC/Getty Images, 6; Prisma/UIG/Getty Images, 10; De Agostini Picture Library/A. Dagli Orti/Bridgeman Images, 11; Radu Bercan/Shutterstock.com, 12; GraphicaArtis/Getty Images, 17; John Elk III/Lonely Planet Images/Getty Images, 18; Alastair Wallace/Shutterstock.com, 21; Lindrik/iStock/Thinkstock.com, 24; Universal History Archive/UIG via Getty Images, 26; Art Media/Print Collector/Getty Images, 32; Renata Sedmakova/Shutterstock.com, 34; Florilegius/SSPL/Getty Images, 35; Art Media/Print Collector/Getty Images, 36; © Tarker/Bridgeman Images, 39; http://wellcomeimages.org/indexplus/obf_images/f6/21/96b5317994bc34d2cc2ddb38d87b.jpg/File:Engraving; German abbess and physician Hildegard von Bingen Wellcome L0005783.jpg/Wikimedia Commons, 42; Castres, bibliothèque municipale/File:Philo mediev.jpg/Wikimedia Commons, 46; Musee Conde, Chantilly, France/Bridgeman Images, 49; David Harris, The Art of Calligraphy, Dorling Kindersley 1995, ISBN 1564588491/File:Book of Hours Bentivoglio.jpg/Wikimedia Commons, 51; Florilegius/SSPL/Getty Images, 53; DeAgostini/Getty Images, 56; Petrusbarbygere/File:Folio 173v - The Entry into Jerusalem.jpg/Wikimedia Commons, 59; David Gee/File:ChesterMysteryPlay 300dpi.jpg/Wikimedia Commons, 60; © Leemage/Bridgeman Images, 62; © Tallandier/Bridgeman Images, 69.

Printed in the United States of America

Contents

INTRODUCTION

THE MEDIEVAL AGE

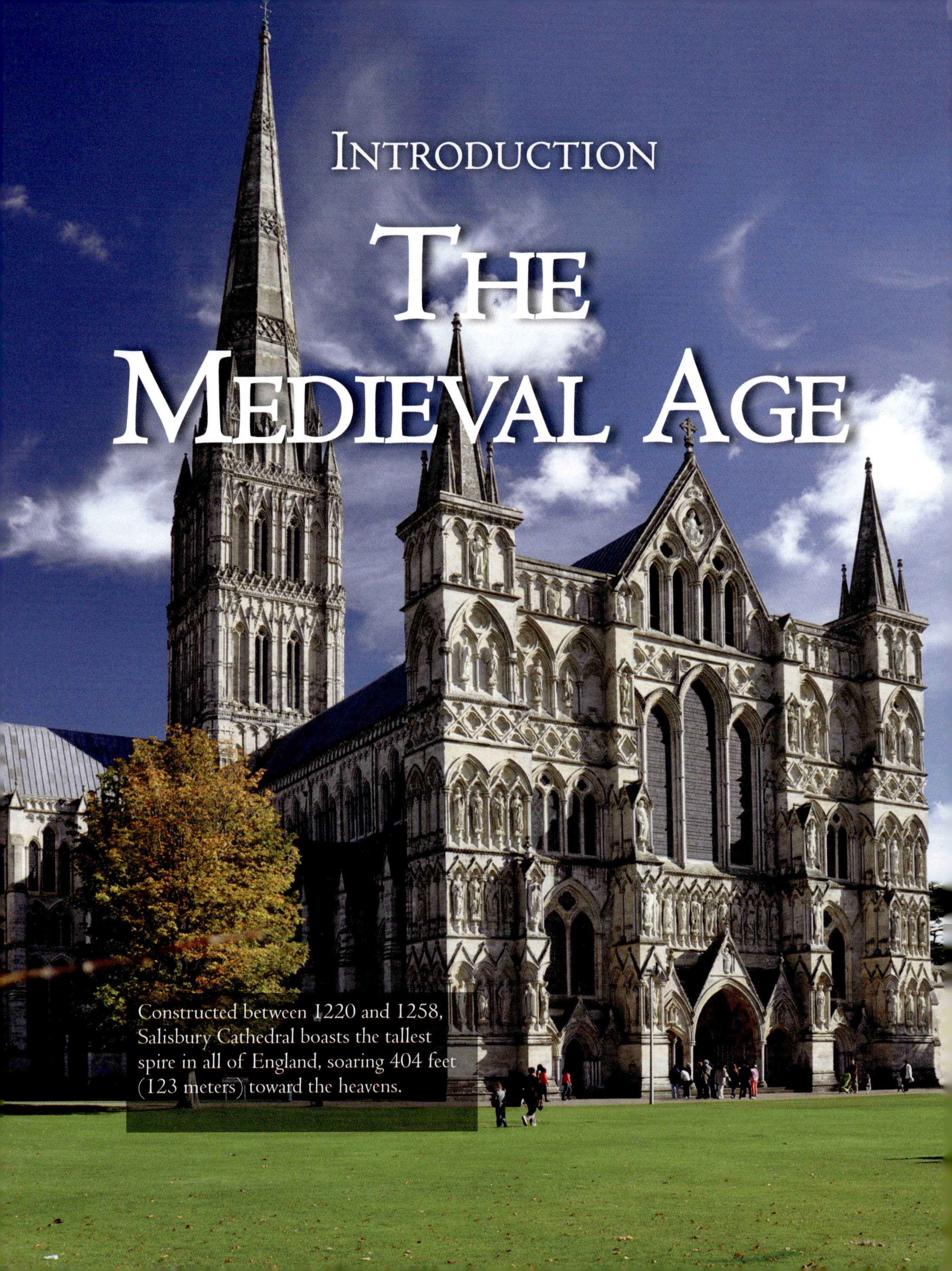

Constructed between 1220 and 1258, Salisbury Cathedral boasts the tallest spire in all of England, soaring 404 feet (123 meters) toward the heavens.

The medieval period, also known as the Middle Ages, spans about one thousand years of European history, between 500 and 1500. The years 1100–1400 made up the High Middle Ages, a period distinguished by a swelling population that led to great social, economic, and political changes across the continent.

The late Middle Ages saw the emergence of **humanists**, individuals who, during the fourteenth century, took a renewed interest in ancient Roman and Greek literature and ideologies. Humanists believed that the previous ten centuries had been a dark age, with no great human advancements or thinkers. They sought to distance themselves from this time period and to create a rebirth of ancient learning. The rise of humanism led to the period following the Middle Ages, which became known as the Renaissance.

During the Middle Ages, the Catholic Church served as a central unifying power across Europe. From his seat in Rome, the pope oversaw an extensive network of religious figures from nuns to **bishops**. From small parish churches to soaring **cathedrals**, the Catholic Church touched the lives of all medieval people.

Chapter One

The Rise of Christianity

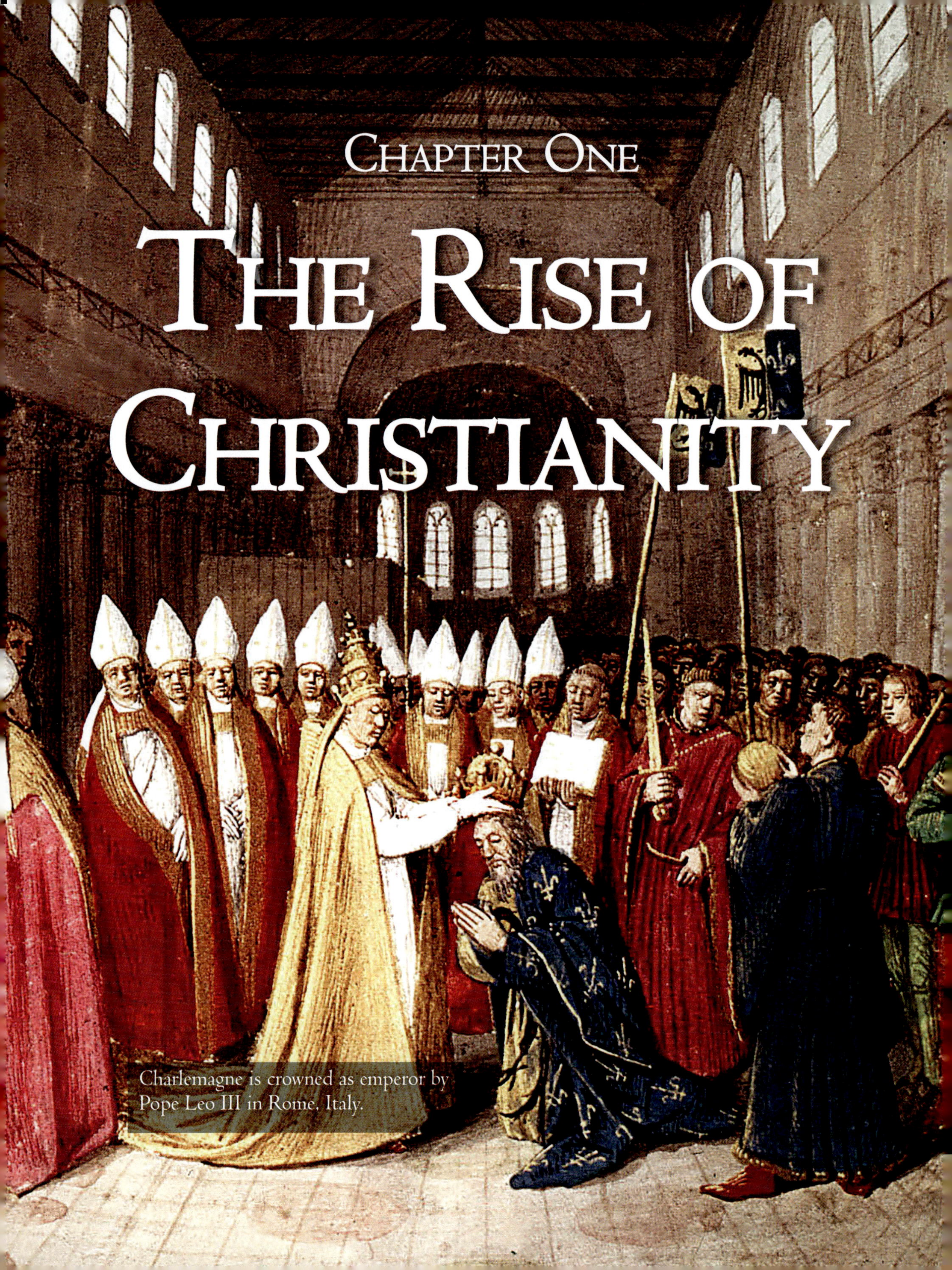

Charlemagne is crowned as emperor by Pope Leo III in Rome, Italy.

"Charles accordingly went to Rome, to set in order the affairs of the Church, which were in great confusion, and passed the whole winter there. It was then that he received the titles of Emperor and Augustus to which he at first had such an aversion that he declared that he would not have set foot in the Church the day that they were conferred, although it was a great feast-day, if he could have foreseen the design of the Pope."

—a description of Charlemagne being crowned emperor on December 25, 800 CE

For centuries, much of Europe was ruled by the Roman Empire. Under Roman rule and the leadership of Emperor Constantine I, Christianity would become the dominant religion of the medieval world.

In the year 313 CE, Roman rule stretched from Spain to the Middle East, including most of western Europe and all of southern Europe. Throughout the empire, people practiced many different religions, including Christianity. At this time, only about 10 percent of western Europe's people were Christians, and Christianity had a much lower status than most other religions. Constantine had been learning a great deal about the new faith, however, and he came to a momentous decision: he would give Christianity equal rights and privileges with other religions. Most of the emperors who came after Constantine were Christians, and they continued to strengthen the church. By the year 400, Christianity was the official religion of the empire.

Beyond the empire's boundaries, among the people whom the Romans called barbarians, ancient religions still flourished. The church, however, believed it had a duty to bring all people into the Christian faith. Since Christianity's beginnings, **missionaries** had traveled far and wide to spread their religion. Now, with the support and protection of the government, the church could send out even more missionaries and spread Christianity even farther.

In the late 400s, the western half of the Roman Empire fell to barbarian invaders. The church remained strong, however, and eventually the invaders converted to Christianity. One Christian descendant of the barbarians was Charles Martel, who turned away a new set of invaders in 732. These were **Muslim** warriors, who for a hundred years had been spreading their religion, **Islam**, from its homeland in Arabia. They had conquered North Africa and advanced up through Spain, but Martel stopped them from going farther into Europe. He became a hero to Christian Europe and founded a line of powerful rulers.

Charles Martel's grandson Charlemagne built a new empire that stretched from France to central Europe. In the year 800, the pope, head of the church, crowned Charlemagne emperor of Rome. Charlemagne's empire did not last long after his death, but the idea of Europe unified by the Catholic Church endured throughout the Middle Ages. The Christian nations of Europe thought of themselves as belonging to the religious realm known as Christendom.

Missionaries continued to spread Christianity, traveling to places as far away as Iceland in the west and Russia in the east. Meanwhile, the eastern half of the old Roman Empire was flourishing as the Byzantine Empire. Its culture differed from that of western Europe in many ways. In particular, the Byzantine churches had serious disagreements with some of the practices and beliefs of the western European churches. In 1054, Christianity split into two factions, which eventually came to be known as the Roman Catholic

Church in the West and the Orthodox Church in the East. By 1300, Catholic Christianity was the official religion of nearly every country in western Europe.

Other European Religions

Not all medieval Europeans were Christians. Several ancient European religions survived well into the Middle Ages. The people of Sweden, for example, still had a temple to the old gods Thor, Odin, and Frey in the twelfth century. Even after the Swedish king declared Christianity his country's official religion, and even after the last temple was closed, some Swedes kept to their traditional beliefs for decades (perhaps even centuries) more. Across the Baltic Sea from Sweden, ancient belief systems held on even longer—the last European state to become officially Christian was Lithuania, in 1386.

European peoples nearly always converted to Christianity "from the top down." First the king would choose to become a Christian, and his nobles would gradually follow suit. With the ruling class's support, the church was then able to start establishing parishes—local or neighborhood churches—throughout the country. Over time, commoners began to adopt Christian beliefs. This was not always a peaceful process, however. The church banned many traditional practices and often harassed people who followed them. Threats and violence were frequently used to force people to become Christians.

While ancient, traditional religions held on in northern Europe, southern Europeans were largely followers of Islam. The kingdom of Granada, in southern Spain, was a Muslim nation until 1492. Many parts of southeastern Europe also became officially Muslim in the mid-1300s. During this period, the Ottoman Empire was expanding from its lands in Turkey, bringing the Muslim faith to all the areas it conquered. Muslim merchants and travelers also spent a great deal of time doing business in European cities such as Venice.

Judaism in Medieval Europe

Medieval cities commonly had sizable Jewish populations, though Jews suffered from many prejudices and restrictions. However, since Christians were generally forbidden to make loans and charge interest, Jews were able to play an important role as bankers and moneylenders in many places.

Jewish moneylenders count out bags of gold coins to serve as loans for Christians.

Governments were often tolerant of Jews, especially when that tolerance proved profitable. All too often during the Middle Ages, however, a ruler needing money would expel the Jews from the area under his control and seize all of their property and belongings. This happened in Paris in 1182; sixteen years later, the banished Jews were allowed to return to the city, but only after paying a tax to the king. Even worse, Jews were sometimes targets of extreme violence; in 1190, 150 Jewish men, women, and children were killed in a riot in the city of York, England. Europe's Christian majority still had a long way to go toward understanding and accepting religious differences.

Religious Practices

Many people have called the Middle Ages the Age of Faith. However, it can be difficult to know how ordinary women and men truly understood their religion. For one thing, church services were given almost entirely in Latin, the official language of the Catholic Church. Sometimes a priest would preach a sermon in the people's everyday language, explaining the Bible and the church's teachings in ways that people could understand. Very few could read the Bible for themselves. It was written in Latin—and besides, the average person could not read at all.

However, the church was strongly supported by most rulers and nobles, and it played a major role in education and the arts. Christian ideas, values, and symbols were present in nearly every facet of society. Also, though there were differences between nations and between social classes, there seems to have been a general feeling among most western Europeans that they were united by Christianity.

Medieval Christians marked important stages of their lives by observing the sacraments of the church. The sacraments were ceremonies that both demonstrated God's grace and bestowed it on those taking part. Soon after birth, a baby was welcomed into the church by the sacrament of baptism. At the sacrament of confirmation, around the age of thirteen, the child made a public commitment to living a Christian life. In the sacrament of confession, or **penance**, a person confessed his or her sins to God through a priest, and the priest assigned a penance for the person to perform to atone for the sins. (The penance often took the form of saying a certain number of prayers.) The other sacrament that every medieval Christian expected to go through was extreme unction. Someone who was thought to be close to death would make a last confession to a priest. After forgiving the confessed sins, the priest anointed the person's body with holy oil in preparation for death.

This painting from the 1800s shows Pope Urban IV hearing the confession of Tannhaeuser, a German knight and poet.

The ceremony of marriage also marked an important milestone in the lives of medieval Christians. For some people, however, marriage was not an option. These pious priests, monks, and nuns dedicated themselves wholly to the Christian faith and serving the church.

Chapter Two

A Christian Europe

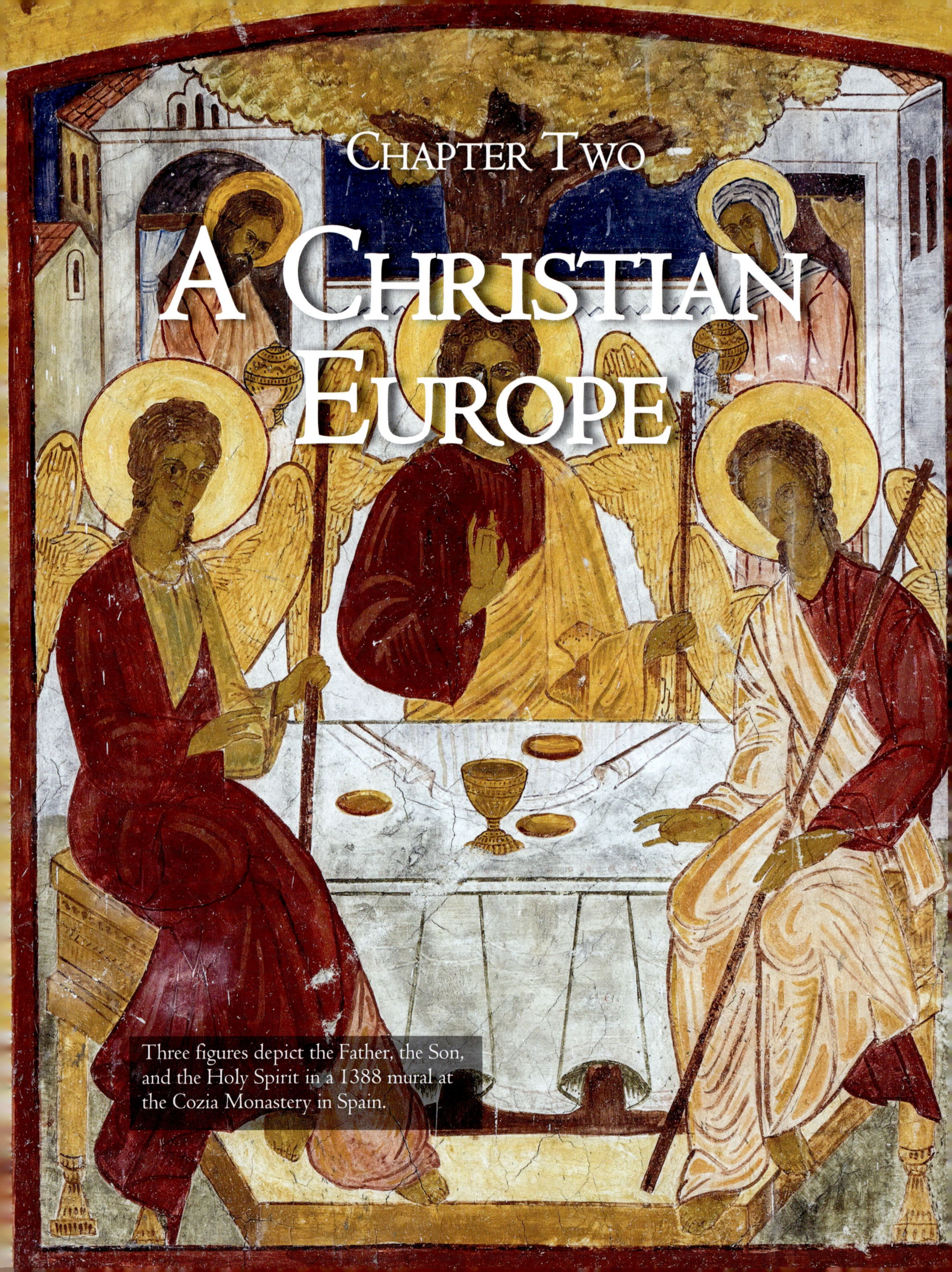

Three figures depict the Father, the Son, and the Holy Spirit in a 1388 mural at the Cozia Monastery in Spain.

"For there are three that bear record in heaven, the Father, the Word, and the Holy Ghost: and these three are one."
—I John 5:7

Christianity is a **monotheistic** religion, as are Islam and Judaism. These religions all share a belief in a single, all-powerful, all-knowing God, who is present everywhere all the time. Christianity teaches that God manifests as three entities, collectively called the Trinity, made up of God the Father, God the Son, and God the Holy Spirit. The life and teachings of the Son, Jesus Christ, form the heart of the Christian faith.

Jesus was a Jew who lived in the kingdom of Judaea (now Israel) from around 4 BCE to 30 CE. The Bible tells that Jesus was born as a human in order to save people from their sins. His mother was Mary, the wife of a carpenter named Joseph. Before Jesus was born, the angel Gabriel visited Mary to tell her that she would become pregnant with a son who would be great and holy. When it was time for the birth, Mary and Joseph were away from home and had to take shelter in a stable. Angels appeared to shepherds nearby to tell them of the holy infant, and a bright star guided wise men from the East to the birthplace. Shepherds and wise men alike knelt in **homage** to the newborn baby.

When Jesus was around thirty years old, he went to his cousin John to be baptized. This was a ceremony in which John symbolically cleansed people of their past sins so that they could begin to live more righteous lives. For the next three years, Jesus traveled through Judaea, performing miracles, healing the sick, and teaching. Many of his lessons centered on the power of love—"You shall love your neighbor as yourself" (Matthew 22:39)—and the importance of the Golden Rule—"Whatever you wish that men would do to you, do so to them" (Matthew 7:12). He also taught that those who believed in him and followed his teachings would have an eternal life in the presence of God. Jesus attracted a large number of followers, both women and men. Twelve of these followers, the **disciples** or apostles, were his most devoted students.

Judaea was part of the Roman Empire, and some people feared that Jesus was trying to start a rebellion and would make himself king of the Jews. He was arrested and put on trial. Condemned to death by the Romans, he was crucified, or executed by being hung on a cross. Three days later, the Bible says, some of his women followers went to his tomb and found it empty. An angel told them that Jesus had been resurrected—he had risen from the dead. After this, Jesus appeared several times to his followers, promising forgiveness of sins and resurrection to all who believed in him. Then he ascended to heaven to rejoin God the Father.

Holy Saints

Like many Christians today, Christians of the Middle Ages honored a large number of **saints**. The saints were people who had lived exceptionally holy lives and who had the power to perform miracles. Saints were believed to dwell in heaven. Although God was the only divine power in the universe, he was often felt to be unreachable. So, if a Christian needed something, she or he might pray to a saint, believing that the saint would then "speak to" God on their behalf.

Patron Saints

People, countries, cities, churches, and organizations of craftspeople usually had one or more patron saints. The patron saint was the special protector of the person or group, who would in turn be especially devoted to this saint. Often a patron saint was chosen because of some similarity between an event in the saint's life and the activities of a particular group. For example, a popular story was told of Saint Crispin, a young Roman nobleman who became a Christian. As he traveled from place to place to preach the new religion, he supported himself as a shoemaker. In one town, he made shoes for many poor people, refusing any payment for his work. At night, angels came and gave him leather to make more shoes for the poor. Because of this, Saint Crispin was regarded as the patron saint of shoemakers and other leatherworkers.

There are several other patron saints: Saint Anne, believed to be the mother of Mary and grandmother of Jesus Christ, is the patron saint of women during childbirth. Saint Joachim, Mary's father, is the patron saint of fathers, grandfathers, grandparents, married couples, cabinet makers, and linen traders. Saint Nicholas, from whom the figure of Santa Claus was based, is the patron saint of many things, including children, sailors, fishermen, and wrongfully convicted criminals.

When seeking a saint's help, a person often prayed before a picture or statue of the saint or, if possible, at a shrine to the saint. Some shrines housed a saint's **relics**, objects associated with the saint or even some of the saint's physical remains (usually bones). Holy relics had a great reputation for miraculous powers.

The most important and best-loved of all the saints was Mary, the mother of Jesus. She had always been important to Christians, but devotion to her grew tremendously during the High Middle Ages. Great churches, cathedrals, and **monasteries** were dedicated to her, such as the cathedrals of Notre Dame in Paris and Chartres, France. ("Notre Dame" means "Our Lady," one of Mary's titles.) Songs were sung in her praise not only in church but also in noble courts. Tales of her life and of the miracles she worked for those who prayed to her were popular in books and with preachers and storytellers, too. One such prayer included the following verse:

> Sweet lady, mother of Jesus Christ,
> For the honour God showed you
> When you left this world
> So full of adversity—
> You ascended truly to heaven,
> And festively your son
> Seated you on the holy throne
> And made you queen of heaven—
> Listen and be ready,
> Lady, to hear my request.
> *Hail Mary*

Mary, also known as the Madonna, is shown with an infant Jesus in a painted panel dating from the 1300s.

Chapter Three

The Church Community

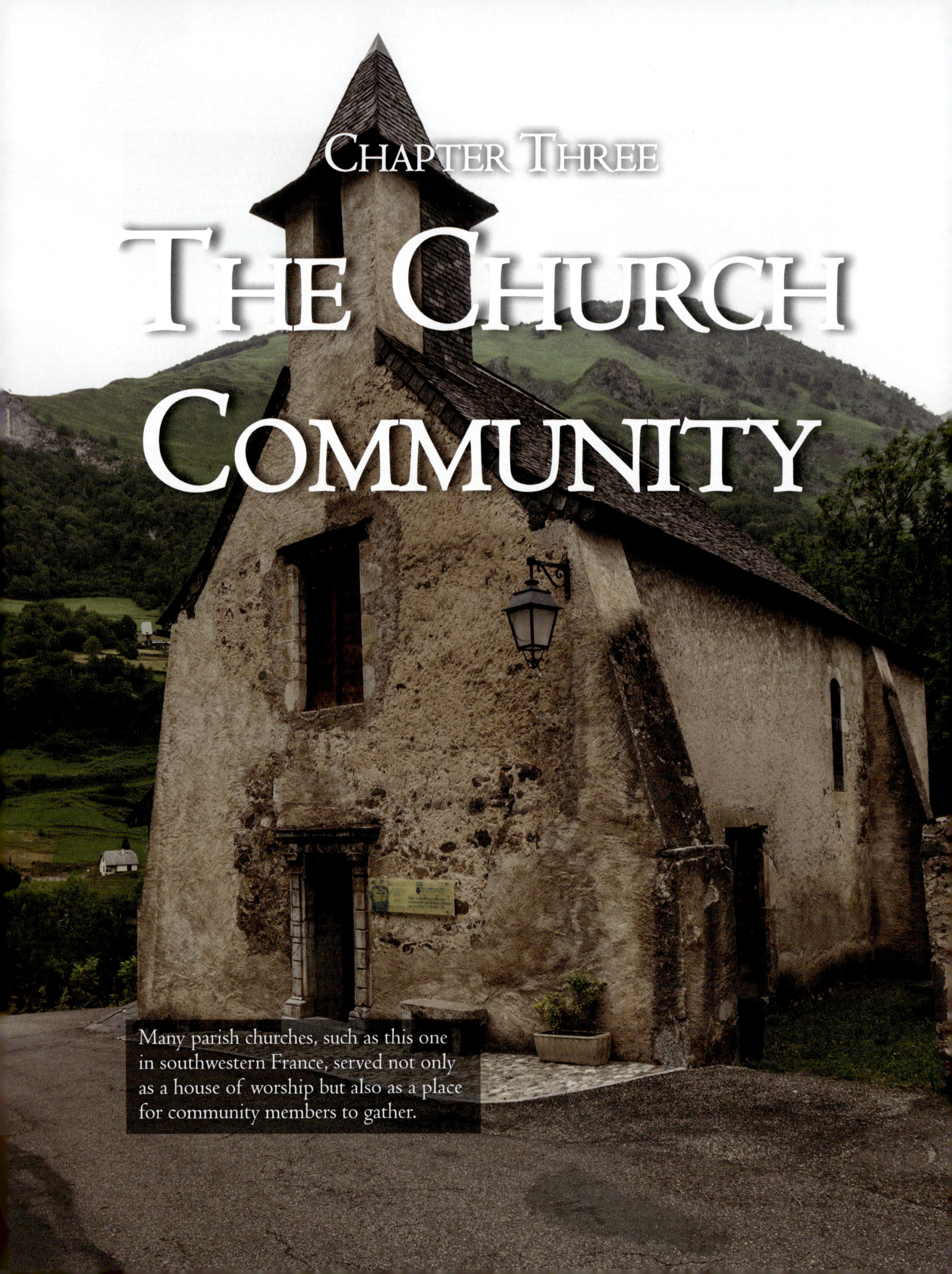

Many parish churches, such as this one in southwestern France, served not only as a house of worship but also as a place for community members to gather.

"Henry de Penketh, forty and more, was at the church to buy corn from Robert Wilkynson.

Henry de Twys, forty and more, was at the church to hear Mass before going to Kirkdale to buy two oxen from Robert Wilkynson of Kirkdale.

William Laghok, forty and more, was at the church to hear Mass before going to Litherland to see a corpse and wreck on the seashore."

—a description of witnesses and their whereabouts during and after the baptism of John de Walton at the parish church in Lancashire, dated 1379

The Catholic Church was a powerful entity. It divided western Europe into parishes. These church communities might be made up of two or three small villages, a single village, or one neighborhood of a larger city or town.

Every parish had its own priest and its own church and cemetery. A number of parishes were grouped together to form a diocese, which was overseen by a bishop. An archbishop had charge of a group of dioceses, called an archdiocese. Above the archbishops were the cardinals, who were counselors and assistants to the pope.

The pope was the bishop of Rome. According to tradition, the first bishop of Rome was Jesus's disciple Saint Peter, whose name means "rock." Before Jesus died, he had said to Peter, "On this rock I will build my church … I will give you the keys of the kingdom of heaven" (Matthew 16:18–19). Because of these statements, the pope, regarded as Saint Peter's successor, was the head of the entire Catholic Church.

Holy Buildings

Most medieval people's religious lives centered around their parish church. In many villages, the church was the only building constructed of stone. It was often a small, plain building, perhaps decorated with a few wall paintings showing scenes from the Bible. Until late in the Middle Ages, there were usually no pews—people had to stand, sit on the floor, or bring stools or benches from home. The parish church also functioned as a kind of community center, a place where meetings and other gatherings could be held.

Cathedrals were the churches where bishops had their headquarters. Located in important cities, they were built to be as large and awe-inspiring as possible. Some cathedrals took more than a hundred years to build. No effort or expense was spared to make them beautiful, to the glory of God and the church.

From tiny village churches to towering cathedrals, most medieval Christian houses of worship were built according to a similar plan. The layout often took the rough shape of a cross.

The most important part of the church was the choir, or chancel. This was always in the east of the building. Here was the high altar, where priests conducted Mass, the main religious service. The altar, made of stone, was on a raised platform reached by three steps, which symbolized the Trinity. At the back of the altar there might be an **altarpiece**—a painting or carved panel showing stories from the life of Jesus or the saints. In cathedrals and other large churches, the altarpiece was usually an elaborate work of art. The choir was only for members of the clergy and often was separated from the main part of the church by a screen carved out of wood or stone.

While the priests chanted the Mass and other services, the people listened from the **nave**. This was the central section of the church. On the north side of the nave there was a pulpit, a kind of raised platform. A priest stood here when

The nave of a towering cathedral housed high ceilings, impressive arches, and artworks showing religious scenes.

he preached a sermon. Some churches also had pulpits built into their outside walls so that preachers could give sermons outdoors.

Behind the choir, large medieval churches often had a place called an ambulatory. Priests and other worshipers could walk up the aisles along the nave and around the ambulatory in religious processions.

Radiating off the ambulatory, there might be several chapels. Chapels could be located in other parts of a church, too. These chapels were semi-enclosed rooms, each with its own altar dedicated to a particular saint. A chapel devoted to the Virgin Mary was called a Lady chapel; a large number of medieval churches had one.

Devoted to God

Parish priests and the churchmen at cathedrals served God and their fellow Christians in the everyday world. However, many religious people in the Middle Ages wished to be able to leave the world behind and turn all their thoughts to God. There were numerous monasteries where they could do this, at least to some extent. A monastery was a place where a group of men or women lived as a community of monks or nuns, devoting themselves to prayer and study. (Today, monasteries for women are usually called convents, or sometimes nunneries.) A few of these communities were **double monasteries**, for both men and women. The monks and nuns lived and worked in separate buildings from each other, but they shared a church and were governed by a single **superior** officer.

A monastery ruled by an abbot (the highest rank of monk) or abbess (the highest rank of nun) was called an **abbey**. It had to have at least twelve monks or nuns. A priory was a monastery headed by a prior or prioress, the second highest rank for monks or nuns. Priories could be smaller than abbeys and were under the authority of abbeys. For example, there were more than three hundred priories dependent on the great abbey of Cluny, France.

Some monasteries were on the outskirts or even in the middle of cities—a prime example of this is Westminster Abbey in London. Other religious communities were in the countryside or in lonely places such as forests or islands. Very often, however, a village or town would grow up outside a monastery's or abbey's walls. When this happened, sometimes the religious community would uproot itself and move to another, more isolated place.

Soaring to the Heavens

Among the most outstanding remains of medieval times are abbeys, churches, and cathedrals. Many of these buildings still serve as places of worship today.

Two basic styles of building were used for medieval houses of worship. The earlier style is now called Romanesque. Like ancient Roman structures, Romanesque buildings featured many rounded arches. In the twelfth century, a new style emerged, which is known as Gothic architecture. Gothic buildings had tall, pointed arches. Thanks to new engineering techniques, stone structures now soared to lofty heights, naturally drawing worshipers' eyes up toward heaven.

The new architecture also allowed large windows to be set into the high walls of the cathedrals and churches. Colored glass was easier to produce at this time than perfectly clear glass, so church designers made a virtue of necessity and created stained glass windows. The first stained glass windows featured simple designs, but artists soon realized that they could make pictures with the glass. Stained glass windows illustrating stories from the Bible and other religious scenes became an important feature of churches.

Cathedrals and other churches were also adorned with sculptures. The portals, or entryways, of cathedrals had particularly impressive sculptures. The tympanum, the arching space above the doorway, was a place where the most important religious scenes were carved. Cathedrals also had sculptures of saints, kings and queens, and imaginary creatures.

Other kinds of artwork could be found as well. Floors, walls, and even ceilings might be decorated with mosaics, tiny pieces of colored tile laid together to form designs or pictures. Choir stalls, where the clergy sat during services, often featured ornate wood carvings. The candlesticks and other objects on the altar could be masterpieces of metalwork.

Paintings decorated many churches. Some of medieval Europe's greatest artworks were painted altarpieces. The walls and ceilings of churches were often painted, too, sometimes very elaborately. For example, between 1290 and 1296, the artist Giotto produced a series of wall paintings about the life of Saint Francis to adorn a new church in Assisi. Such paintings helped bring biblical figures, saintly role models, and Christian teachings to life for all worshipers.

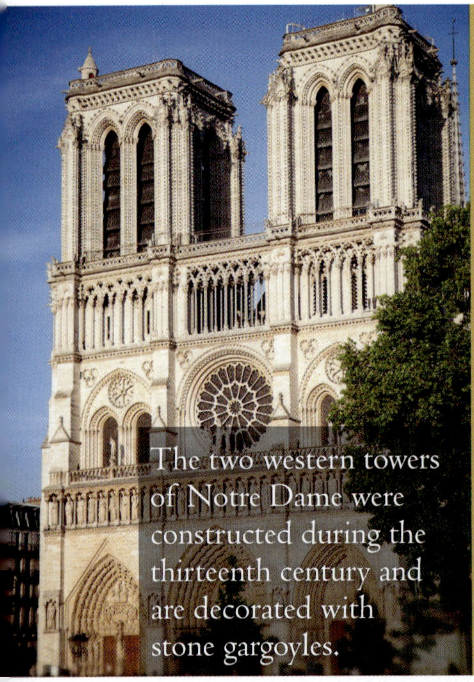

The two western towers of Notre Dame were constructed during the thirteenth century and are decorated with stone gargoyles.

Notre Dame Cathedral

Notre Dame in Paris, France, is the best-known example of medieval Gothic architecture. Construction of the cathedral began under the leadership of Pope Alexander III in 1163 on the Île de la Cité, an island on the River Seine. Work continued on the imposing stone structure until about 1250. As construction continued, flying buttresses were added to support the upper structure. The cathedral's two towers stand 223 feet (68 m) high. Three rose windows made of beautiful stained glass survive from the thirteenth century.

The center of a monastery was its **cloister**. A cloister is a square or rectangular covered walkway around a garden or open area. Many cloisters were enclosed, with glass windows looking out on the garden. Monks and nuns might spend hours each day in such a cloister, which often had alcoves where they could sit to read, pray, or meditate. The stone floors of these cloisters were strewn with sweet-smelling rushes, and in cold weather, **braziers** could be set up for warmth.

From the cloister, monks and nuns could get to other important rooms and buildings, such as the monastery's church. There was also a **chapter house**, the business center of the monastery. The **refectory** was the building where monks and nuns had their meals. Just outside the refectory might be a lavatorium, a place for washing up. Nearby was the community's kitchen.

Monastery residents slept in a dormitory. This was either a large open room with a number of beds, or a room divided into small cells, each containing little more than a bed. A "night stair" often led from the dormitory directly to the church so that the residents could easily attend nighttime services.

Large monasteries might have many other buildings besides those around the cloister. The superior (the monk or nun who was the head of the monastery) sometimes had a separate house. There could be workshops for different crafts, stables for horses, barns, a mill for grinding grain, and guest houses. Guests entered the monastery through a gatehouse. This was also a place where poor people came to receive food, clothing, and other assistance from the monks or nuns.

Many abbeys drew their wealth from farming and other ventures outside the monastery's walls. The income generated from their avenues supported the work of the church, its aid to the poor, and the creation of great religious buildings, artworks, and writings.

Chapter Four

A Pious Life

Many monks were able to write. Most of the surviving manuscripts from the medieval age were created by these pious men.

"And the ladder thus set up is our life in the world,
which the Lord raises up to heaven if our heart is humbled.
For we call our body and soul the sides of the ladder,
and into these sides our divine vocation has inserted
the different steps of humility and discipline we must climb."
—from *The Rule of St. Benedict,* Chapter 7: On Humility

Within the church, there were roles and levels of power that a man could hold as a man of God. Some men remained in the lower ranks while others went on to hold positions of leadership that could lead to great power and responsibility.

Men who took holy orders, dedicating themselves to the religious life, became members of the clergy. The **secular** clergy were those who were out in the world, interacting with people on a day-to-day basis. They might be parish priests, bishops, or cathedral officials. The regular clergy were those who lived according to a set of guidelines called a **rule** (*regula* in Latin). The regular clergy, mainly monks, usually lived apart from the world. Monks could also be priests, and many were.

Ranks of Clergy

There were several grades of secular clergy. The lowest ones were called the minor orders. Originally they each had specific duties, but by the High

Middle Ages they were mainly stages in the education of a priest. Some men remained in minor orders all their lives, though. Their training enabled them to take up important positions in government and in noble households, among other things. A noble's treasurer, for example, was very often a cleric in minor orders. Other clerics in minor orders might teach in schools or universities.

It generally took many years of study and devotion to become a priest. Once a man reached the major orders, the higher grades of clergy, he began to take on definite responsibilities in religious services. Finally, at the age of twenty-five, having moved through all the other orders, a man could become a priest. As a priest, he was empowered to offer Holy Communion (the most important part of Mass), to preach, to bless, and to forgive sins. He could administer all the sacraments except confirmation and holy orders. If he was a parish priest, his main duty was to use these powers to care for the souls of the people of his parish. Someday, through hard work and good fortune, he might become a bishop. Then he would be able to administer all the sacraments, and he would become responsible for the supervision and care of all the priests in his diocese.

Although the secular clergy lived and worked among the people, they were set off from them in important ways. The visible sign of the clergy's dedication to religion was the **tonsure**, a special haircut that left the top of the head bald. Clergymen were not required to serve in the military or to pay taxes. They were forbidden to engage in buying and selling, loaning money, and similar trades. They were allowed, however, to work outside the church to earn their living if necessary. They were also instructed to avoid gambling, hunting, and other unsuitable pastimes. People in holy orders, if accused of crimes, could only be tried by the church's courts.

Clerics in the major orders were not supposed to marry. However, until the twelfth century it was fairly common for a country priest to have a wife and children. This seems to have been accepted by the local peasants, but church authorities frowned on it. Eventually the church established severe penalties for married clergymen and their wives and children. Church leaders feared that priests with wives and children would be distracted by family life from focusing all of their time and energy to God's service.

Living a Holy Life

Almost from the beginnings of Christianity, there had been people who wanted to withdraw from the world and turn all their attention to God. Many such people went out into wilderness areas and lived alone as hermits. Others gathered together in small communities devoted to the religious life; these were the first monasteries. Around the year 529, Saint Benedict founded a new monastery in Italy. Benedict wrote a book of rules to guide his monks. *The Rule of Saint Benedict* became the basis of monastery life for centuries to come.

All monks vowed themselves, for the rest of their lives, to poverty (they were not allowed to own any personal property), chastity (they could not marry or have relationships with women), and obedience (to the head of the monastery and to the church's teachings). The Benedictine Rule gave further guidance to their lives. It covered everything from what sort of man should be chosen abbot and how religious services should be conducted to how much the monks should eat and what their clothing should be made of. All of this was designed to help the monks think of God and the monastery community before themselves. Everything was owned in common, by the monastery as a whole. Clothing, food, and tools were distributed to each monk according to his need.

The abbot was the supreme authority in any monastery. His deputy was the prior. In an abbey, the prior assisted the abbot, while in a priory, he supervised the monks on the abbot's behalf. In both abbeys and priories, one monk was appointed as cellarer. His job was to oversee the monks' food supplies; if the monastery was a large one, he was allowed to have several assistants. The porter was an elderly monk who lived in a cell near the monastery door. It was his responsibility to admit guests and to distribute food and clothing to the needy when they came to the monastery. Another important position in many monasteries was that of infirmarian. This monk was in charge of taking care of the sick, usually with the help of medicinal herbs grown in the monastery garden. Some monasteries gave treatment not only to their residents but also to local poor people. There were other offices as well, especially in large monasteries, but no matter what position a monk held, he was always expected to be humble about it.

In spite of the Benedictine Rule's emphasis on humility, simplicity, and separation from the world, many abbeys became so large, wealthy, and powerful that some monks decided they needed to make reforms. In 1098, Saint Robert of Molesme founded a new abbey at Cîteaux (see-TOH), France, and demanded that his monks return to strictly following the Benedictine Rule. This began a movement that spread throughout Europe in the twelfth century and resulted in the creation of a new religious society, the Cistercian Order. Several other orders were created and flourished during this time, too, but the Cistercian Order was the largest and most influential.

The Cistercians gave a prominent role to **lay brothers**. These were men who took the same vows as the monks but did not participate in the daily religious services, which monks were required to do. Instead, the lay brothers were responsible for cooking, cleaning, grinding grain, making repairs, constructing buildings, and making such things as candles, **parchment** (animal skin specially prepared for writing on), and blankets and clothing. The lay brothers also did a great deal of farmwork, raising crops and livestock both to supply the monks and to sell for the support of the monastery. Their work allowed Cistercian monasteries to be entirely self-sufficient and cut off from the world.

Lay brothers usually lived in their own building at the monastery, but many Cistercian abbeys owned widely scattered farms, called granges. The lay brothers who did the farmwork lived at the granges. Each farm was in the charge of a lay brother with the title "master of the grange." No matter how far the grange was from its abbey, the master of the grange and the other lay brothers were usually expected to return to the abbey for Sunday services every week and for services on important holidays.

In the Footsteps of the Disciples

In the first part of the thirteenth century, a new wave of religious feeling produced new kinds of religious societies. These were called the mendicant orders, from the Latin word that means "begging," because their members embraced total poverty and were supported completely by charity. The main mendicant orders were the Franciscans, founded by Saint Francis of Assisi, and the Dominicans, founded by Saint Dominic. Members of these orders were called **friars**, meaning "brothers."

Saint Francis was the son of a wealthy Italian cloth merchant. As a young man, Francis was a soldier and lived a life of pleasure, caring more for fine clothes than for God. Still, he was always generous to the poor. Then, during the course of a battle, he was captured, and for a year he remained a prisoner of war. The experience changed him. More and more, his thoughts turned to religion. After a time, his holiness and charity began to attract followers.

In church one day, Francis heard the Gospel reading in which Jesus instructs his disciples to go out into the world "and preach as you go, saying, 'The kingdom of heaven is at hand.' Heal the sick, raise the dead, cleanse lepers, cast out demons. You received without pay, give without pay. Take no gold, nor silver, nor copper in your belts, no bag for your journey, nor two tunics, nor sandals, nor a staff" (Matthew 10: 7–10). This was exactly what Francis wanted to do, and he was inspired to write a rule for himself and his followers. They gave away everything they owned and traveled from place to place, taking with them nothing but the simple, rough woolen robes on their backs. Everywhere they went, they preached and helped the poor. Eventually the Franciscans had many monasteries, where they lived very simply—but never permanently, for it was always their mission to be out among the people, following in the steps of Jesus's disciples.

St. Francis sought to embody the teachings of Jesus through his humble rule and selfless actions. He is the patron saint of animals, merchants, and ecology.

Saint Dominic was inspired by this example. The order he founded also had a mission to send preachers out among the people. The Dominicans' special concerns were to improve people's morals and to make certain their beliefs were in line with official church teachings. Dominicans were often highly educated, with a thorough knowledge of the church's history and laws, so that they could be effective preachers.

The Canons

A middle way between the secular and regular clergy was occupied by men known as canons. They lived by a rule that medieval people believed was set down by Saint Augustine in the fifth century. At the same time, they were "in the world," for they, too, were trying to follow in the footsteps of the disciples, in particular by doing good works among the people. Many groups of canons ran hospitals, to help the poor. Canons could also serve as parish priests.

Most canons lived in houses together. These houses were usually in cities, but occasionally they could be in very isolated places. Some canons, known as secular canons, did not give up personal property but lived in homes of their own. These canons were generally associated with managing the affairs of cathedrals and often ran schools.

Riding to Battle

The Catholic Church taught that all people were basically sinful but that acts of penance could earn forgiveness for sin. One of the most powerful acts of penance was going on a **pilgrimage**, a journey to an important religious site. The greatest pilgrimage was to Jerusalem, the scene of Jesus's death and resurrection.

The Crusades

In 1095, the pope sent out a call for **knights** to go to Jerusalem to take the city from its Muslim rulers. This was the beginning of the First Crusade, a pilgrimage and at the same time a war fought for God.

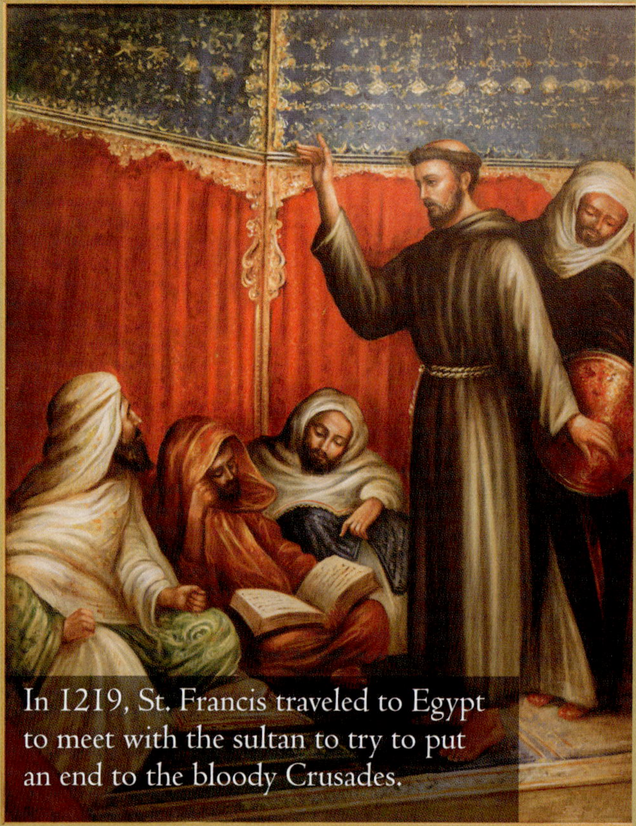

In 1219, St. Francis traveled to Egypt to meet with the sultan to try to put an end to the bloody Crusades.

The word "crusade" is derived from the Latin word *crux*, meaning "cross." In 1071, control of much of the Holy Land, including the sacred city of Jerusalem, fell into the hands of a group of Muslims whom did not welcome Christians on pilgrimage.

For over two hundred years, many wars were fought between Christians and Muslims for control over the Holy Land in the Middle East. The crusaders won Jerusalem and other parts of the Holy Land, where they established their own kingdoms. Many Europeans settled there. Some of them formed groups dedicated to protecting and caring for the pilgrims who came in growing numbers now that Jerusalem was in Christian hands. These groups eventually became religious orders of knights. By 1200 there were two major orders: the Knights Templars and the Knights Hospitallers.

In both the Knights Templars and the Knights Hospitallers, full members took the lifelong monastic vows of poverty, chastity, and obedience. They lived in communities and followed a rule. The Templars' rule was based on that of Saint Benedict, while the Hospitallers followed the Rule of Saint Augustine. There were four classes of members: brothers knight, brothers sergeant (less heavily armed, lower-ranking warriors), brothers at service (who were not fighters), and chaplains (the orders' priests). When knights and sergeants were not out fighting the Muslims, they were expected to participate in the full round of daily religious services or to say a set number of prayers every day. Most of the rest of their time was probably spent in military training.

A member of the Knights Templar was easily recognizable in his white tunic marked with a red cross.

In the Middle East, Templars and Hospitallers lived in castles that served as both a fortress and a monastery. The military orders eventually had many members in Europe, too. Here they lived in smaller communities, known as commanderies. In some cities, such as London, the Templars and Hospitallers had large, grand churches, which for many people symbolized the holy city of Jerusalem itself.

Chapter Five

Medieval Nuns

As brides of Christ, nuns made a lifelong commitment to the church and its teachings.

this was in addition to supervising the nuns and chaplains of her monasteries. In a double monastery, such as the Abbey of Fontevrault (fohn-teh-VROH) in France, even the monks might be under the rule of an abbess.

Life in the Monastery

Many nuns were brought to the monastery as children to prepare for a life in God's service. Here, a nun places a head covering called a habit on a young girl.

Most women's monasteries followed the Rule of Saint Benedict and were run almost exactly like the men's Benedictine monasteries. The monastery's offices were the same, only filled by women: abbess, prioress, cellaress, and so on. However, in Cistercian communities, **lay sisters** did not have quite the same role as lay brothers. Instead of spending time living and working at monastic granges, lay sisters remained in the monastery. There, like lay brothers, they did much of the monastery's physical and practical work so that the nuns could be free for religious services, prayer, and study.

In the mendicant orders, the roles of women were very different from those of male members. Both Saint Francis and Saint Dominic personally founded monasteries for women. However, both agreed—as did church

A Solitary Life

Some nuns chose to live a solitary life of religious devotion, apart from the monastery community. These women were known as anchoresses. They lived in small cells "anchored" to the church, called an anchorage. The anchorage was fitted with three windows: one through which to receive Holy Communion, one through which to communicate with her assistant, and one through which visitors could seek her counsel.

Julian of Norwich is the best-known anchoress from the medieval period. She was born in around 1342. After falling ill in 1373, Julian was healed and received a series of sixteen visions of Jesus and the Virgin Mary. She wrote about these visions in two writings, one short and the other much lengthier. The work is known as the *Revelations of Divine Love* and is considered one of the most important religious texts of the Middle Ages. A modern English adaptation from the fifth chapter reads:

> And in this he showed me a little thing, the quantity of a hazelnut, lying in the palm of my hand, it seemed, and it was as round as any ball. I looked thereupon with the eye of my understanding, and I thought, 'What may this be?' And it was answered generally thus: 'It is all that is made.' I wondered how it could last, for I thought it might suddenly fall to nothing for little cause. And I was answered in my understanding: 'It lasts and ever shall, for God loves it; and so everything has its beginning by the love of God.' In this little thing I saw three properties; the first is that God made it; the second is that God loves it; and the third is that God keeps it.

authorities—that women should not follow in the footsteps of the apostles as wandering preachers. Like other nuns, female members of the Franciscan and Dominican orders were not supposed to leave their monasteries, so they could not work among the poor as their brother monks did. However, they did give food and clothing to any poor people who came to the monastery gatehouse for help. Also, like nuns of other orders, sometimes they could serve the outside world by running schools for children (though usually only children of the upper classes).

Among the People

Many women thrived under the seclusion and discipline of a monastery. They appreciated the opportunity to devote themselves to prayer and study and the freedom from marriage and childbearing. Other women sought a more active religious life, not so completely separated from the world. Some also wished to serve God but not to take the lifetime vows of nuns.

Canonesses were women who lived in a religious community run according to the Rule of Saint Augustine. They did not give up personal property, and they could return to "the world" whenever they wished. They vowed chastity and obedience for the time they lived in the community, but they did not have to keep these vows after they left. Canonesses might also live in their own homes, continuing to follow the Augustinian Rule.

The Franciscans and Dominicans both recognized that there were many women who wished to dedicate themselves to religion but could not join monasteries because they were already married (or sometimes for other reasons). These women could become tertiaries, members of what was sometimes called the Franciscan or Dominican Third Order. Tertiaries lived in their own homes. Married men could also become tertiaries, under the same

Abbess Hildegard

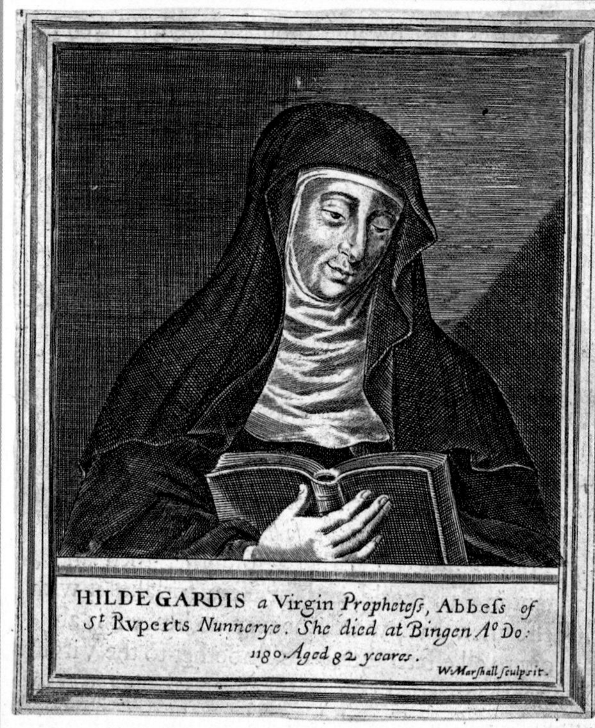

In 1105 a seven-year-old German girl was taken to a small monastery to receive a religious education. The girl, Hildegard, learned scripture, music, and Latin. At the age of fourteen, she took vows and became a nun. Over the years, she gained the respect of her fellow nuns, and at the age of thirty-eight they elected her as their abbess.

Hildegard had had religious visions since childhood. When she was forty-two, she had a vision in which the heavens opened up and flooded her brain with a brilliant light. The light warmed her all through, and she instantly understood the deepest meanings of scripture. As the experience ended, God commanded her to write down all of her visions from then on. At first, Hildegard was reluctant because she doubted herself. However, after a long illness, she began to record her religious experiences, often dictating them to her secretary, a monk named Volmar.

In Hildegard's time, many people sought to have mystical experiences like she did. They wanted to experience God in a direct and personal way and to see visions that revealed his purposes and his glory. Church authorities were often suspicious of mystics, though, because sometimes their visions were not in line with official teachings. Hildegard was very anxious about this. She wrote to the great and influential Cistercian monk Bernard of Clairvaux (clair-VOH) to ask for his blessing. Bernard, in turn, showed some chapters of Hildegard's first book to the pope. The pope wrote to her, full of admiration and praise. From this point on, Hildegard never doubted herself.

Hildegard's monastery was growing, and around the year 1150, she moved it to Rupertsberg, near Bingen, Germany. Eventually she had fifty nuns and two chaplains under her rule. Even more people came under her influence. She became famous not only in Germany but also in France, Flanders (now Belgium), England, Italy, and even Greece. Large numbers of people wrote to her for her advice. Over the rest of her life, she corresponded with various abbesses, bishops, university professors, and nobles, and also with several queens and kings, two emperors, four popes, and at least two future saints (Bernard of Clairvaux and Thomas à Becket).

Along with her visionary works, Hildegard wrote books that dealt with science, philosophy, medicine, and natural history. She was also gifted musically. She was one of medieval Europe's greatest composers of religious chants, writing hymns and other religious music. She composed some musical plays, too, which the nuns of her monastery probably performed. Hildegard described music as a way of recapturing the original beauty and joy of paradise.

Hildegard of Bingen was eighty-one when she died in 1179. In her last years, she wrote of the light that she always saw in her spirit and the living light that was the love of God. During her long life, she was able to shine that light upon many others, and to make the most of opportunities that few other medieval women enjoyed.

conditions, and it sometimes happened that both a man and his wife would decide to take the vows of tertiaries. They still lived together, but as brother and sister instead of as husband and wife.

Canonesses and women tertiaries frequently dedicated themselves to caring for the sick. They might work alongside monks in hospitals such as Paris's famous Hôtel de Dieu ("hostel of God"). During the Middle Ages, hospitals cared for the poor, and often for orphans and widows, as well as the sick. By doing these good works, many canonesses and tertiaries felt they were following in the footsteps of the disciples in ways that nuns in monasteries never could.

The Beguines

There was another kind of religious life for women, created by women themselves. Beginning in the late twelfth century, in what is now Belgium, groups of women known as Beguines chose to dedicate themselves to religion in a new way. They did not enter monasteries or make lifetime vows. They lived simply but did not embrace poverty. They could also choose to marry.

The Beguine movement spread from Belgium to Germany and France. There were many differences among the various groups of Beguines, but they all had a common desire to live the way Jesus and his disciples had lived: not only spending lots of time in prayer but also working among the poor and sick. Some Beguines were so enthusiastic about the religious life that they preached sermons and debated religious issues publicly—activities forbidden to women by the church. There were other Beguines who defied church law and translated the Bible from Latin into German and French so that ordinary people could read it.

The first Beguines were mostly from noble or rich merchant families.

The movement soon attracted numerous working and poor women. Many women in these lower classes desired a religious life, but most could not afford to join monasteries, and many did not want to be so totally cut off from the rest of human society. Beguines spent much of their days in prayer and helping the poor, but they also usually worked for their living. Spinning, weaving, sewing, doing laundry, and caring for the sick were the most common trades worked by Beguines. In addition, some Beguines ran schools in various medieval cities.

At first, Beguines lived in their own or their parents' homes. Gradually, groups of Beguines began to live together in houses, dividing their days between work, prayer, and charity. The late thirteenth century saw the creation of large beguinages, which were almost miniature cities. The Great Beguinage in the Belgian city of Ghent, for example, included more than a hundred houses, two churches, a hospital, and a brewery.

While many people admired the work of the Beguines, some members of the church did not support these communities. Suspicious of their independence, the church began to break up the beguinages.

Chapter Six

A Religious Childhood

Two young pupils receive lessons from a monk.

"Play leads to sorrow. Sometimes it promises laughter and gaiety, but more often brings forth sadness."
—William of Canterbury, a Benedictine monk

People joined the church at all ages and from all levels of society. Some, particularly lay brothers and sisters, entered religious service as adults. Others were raised in the church from birth.

If a woman's husband died, she might go to live in a monastery instead of remarrying or living as a widow. There were also men who joined monasteries when their wives died. Many of these widows and widowers had always been deeply religious, like Saint Birgitta (or Bridget) of Sweden, who founded a double monastery after her husband's death. Others, like Eleanor of Aquitaine, the queen of England, retired to monasteries in order to live quieter, protected lives, but did not make any religious vows.

Most priests, monks, and nuns, however, began their life in the church when they were children. Although many had humble origins, most were children of nobles and wealthy city dwellers. Usually their parents had made the decision to dedicate them to religion. This happened frequently in the case of younger sons, who by law would not inherit the family property. Younger daughters, too, were often marked for a religious life, since many families could provide dowries for only one or two daughters to marry. Parents would occasionally promise God that they would dedicate a child to the religious life even before the baby was born, but the decision was generally made several years later.

It was also common for nobles to send physically or mentally handicapped children to monasteries. This may sound heartless—and numerous churchmen objected to the practice—but in medieval Europe, many of these children would not have been able to support themselves as adults. In a monastery, they would be cared for their entire lives. Orphaned children, too, were commonly dedicated to religious service. Usually the orphan's guardians believed this was the best way to give the child a secure future. Occasionally, however, the guardians simply wanted to help themselves to the child's inheritance.

Sometimes older children or teenagers felt a strong calling to go into the religious life, even if their parents did not wish them to. For noble sons who did not want to be knights and for wealthy merchants' sons who did not want to go into business, entering the church was also a sensible way to earn a living. For upper-class girls who did not want to marry, becoming a nun was the only respectable alternative to becoming a wife and mother. It was also very often their only opportunity to pursue an education and use their talents. However, whether young people joined the church because of the desire for freedom and opportunity, for practical reasons, or because of devotion to God—or for all these reasons—they sometimes had great difficulty with their families because of their decision. Nevertheless, it was the nuns and churchmen who chose the religious life for themselves who were generally happiest and most successful in the church.

A Monastic Upbringing

A manuscript illustration shows young boys and girls entering the religious life at the Clairvaux monastery. The monks are recognizable by their tonsure haircuts.

Boys who entered monasteries had a difficult period of adjustment and training. They were constantly supervised by a senior monk, their teacher. They were never left by themselves or in groups of only children. They could not signal or speak to one another without the teacher's permission. In many places, they were allowed to play for only one hour once a week or once a month. In some monasteries, they were not allowed to play at all.

Girls being raised and educated in monasteries seem to have been allowed a little more playtime. (One reason for this may be that girls usually entered monasteries when they were five or six years old, much younger than most boys did.) Otherwise, they had the same restrictions as boys. They did not always receive the same education, though. They did learn to read and write, and of course they were thoroughly instructed in religion. Few girls, however, had the opportunity to master Latin or to study such subjects as science and law. On the other hand, many received training as scribes and artists, and there were women's monasteries that were well known for the books they produced.

Children in monasteries were expected to be respectful and disciplined. They attended all of the daily religious services, just as the adult monks and nuns did, though sometimes children were allowed to lie down on their seats, while the adults had to remain sitting upright.

According to church law, young people who were educated in monasteries were free to decide not to become monks or nuns and could choose to leave the community after turning twelve. However, this rarely happened. Most monastery-raised children made their vows of poverty, chastity, and obedience between the ages of thirteen and sixteen and spent the rest of their lives in religious service.

Religious Studies

For boys who would become priests, religious education typically started around age seven. At this point, a boy might receive his first tonsure, marking his entrance into holy orders. Now he would go to school to begin his training. He might attend a monastery school or one run by the local parish church or cathedral.

The school day was ten or twelve hours long, from just after sunup to just before sundown. The children sat on hard benches listening to the teacher, reading, and reciting their lessons. There were only two breaks in the long day: an hour in the morning and an hour at lunchtime. Discipline was strict, and it was acceptable for teachers to whip students for misbehaving.

In elementary school, students learned to read both Latin and their everyday language. They were also taught some arithmetic and writing, along with prayers, hymns, and basic Christian beliefs. In some places, girls were able to attend elementary school alongside boys.

At the age of ten or twelve, boys could go on to grammar school. Here they received intense training in Latin so that they would be able to write and speak it fluently. They also learned the art of public speaking, a little science and law, and some music. They studied important books of philosophy, religion, and ancient literature. By the end of grammar school, they were supposed to have a thorough knowledge of the Bible and the church's teachings.

Reading and Writing

Some boys concentrated on the art of handwriting. After mastering the difficult skill of writing on parchment with a quill pen, they would become scribes. In the era before the printing press was invented, all books were completely handmade, and scribes were very important. They made new copies of old books and wrote out new books that authors dictated to them.

Within the monastery, books were stored in a library. A special room, called a scriptorium, was attached to the library. Here, scribes wrote and copied manuscripts. In the poorly lit scriptorium, monks worked silently, copying manuscripts. The work was detailed and time-consuming. Higher ranking members of the clergy might have had their own private cells for religious study and writing.

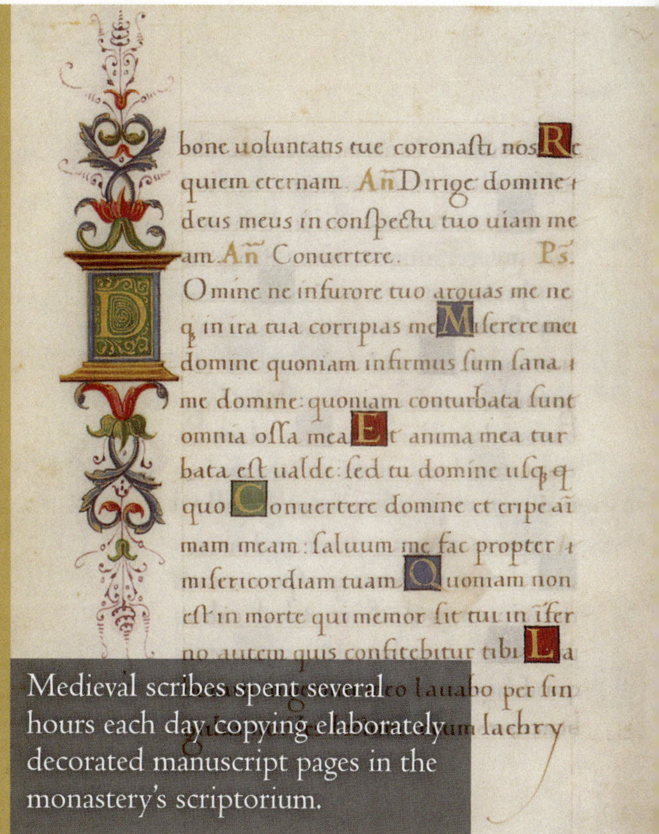

Medieval scribes spent several hours each day copying elaborately decorated manuscript pages in the monastery's scriptorium.

Between the ages of fourteen and sixteen, a boy could begin attending a university. Here he would pursue in-depth study of literature, philosophy, religious thinking, and sometimes law. A university education was not required for all priests, but most bishops had this higher education.

Most monks followed this educational path, although some went to elementary and sometimes grammar school before joining a monastery. Even after becoming monks, they might continue their studies by attending one of the universities that emerged during the medieval age. Some monastic orders, such as the Franciscans and Dominicans, ran their own schools for their members.

Chapter Seven

Labors in the Name of the Lord

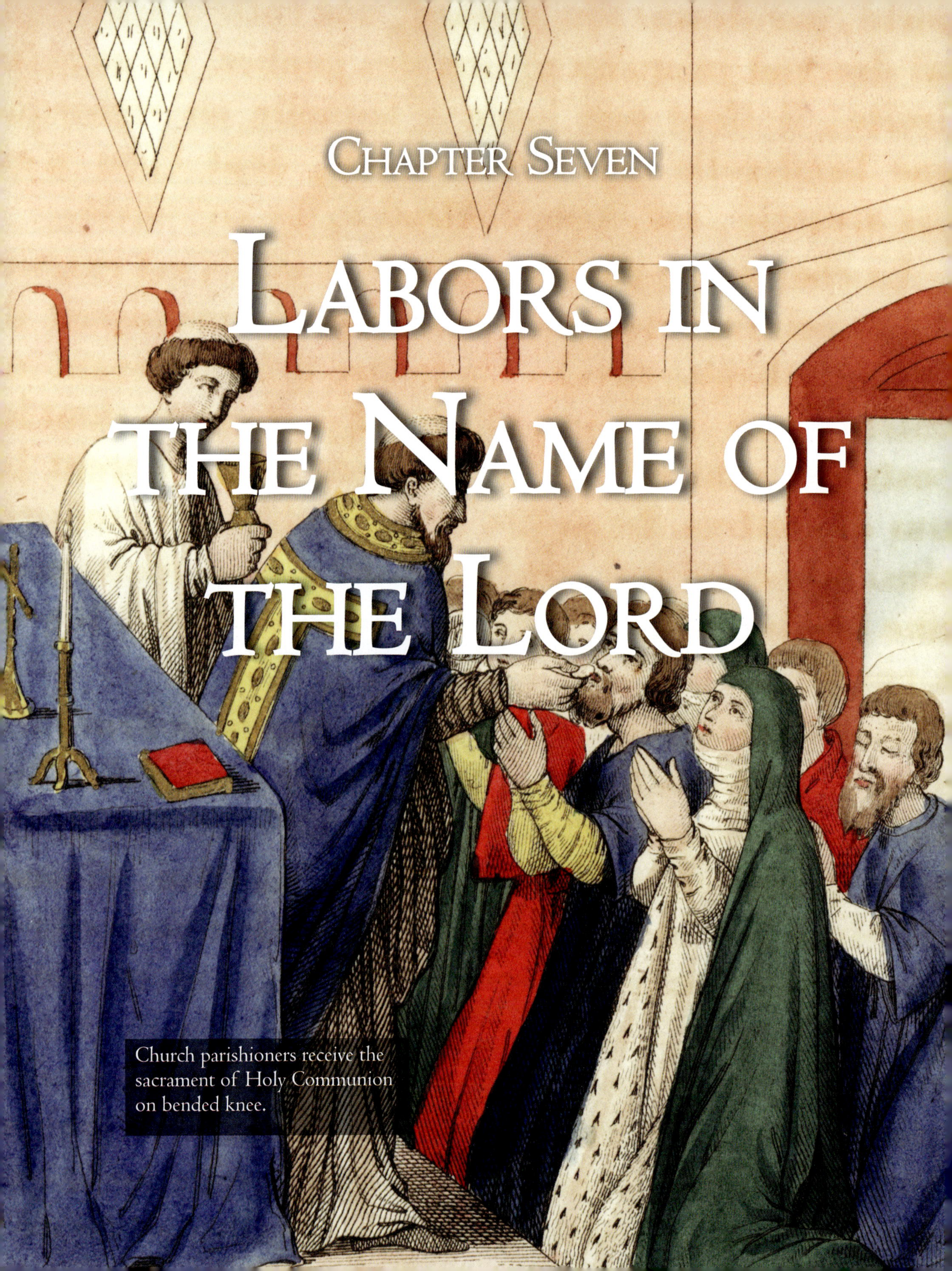

Church parishioners receive the sacrament of Holy Communion on bended knee.

"Now the farmer labours for our food and the warrior must fight against our enemies and the servant of God must continually pray for us and fight spiritually against the unseen foes. It is therefore a mighty fight the monks wage against the unseen devils who plot against us while men of this world fight with worldly weapons against earthly foes."
—Ælfric of Eynsham (circa 955–1010)

There were three divisions of medieval society: those who worked, those who held power and ruled, and those who prayed.

The clergy, of course, belonged to the third group, and prayer was the center of their lives, especially for those in monasteries. Some prayer was private, but most of it took place during regular church services.

In all churches, there were religious services held throughout the day, every day. The main service was Mass. Its most important part was Holy Communion. This sacrament was modeled on the Last Supper, Jesus's final meal with his disciples. He had given them bread and wine, telling them that these were his body and blood, and bid them eat and drink in memory of him. At Communion, the priest gave specially blessed wafers, called the Host, to the congregation, saying, "Hoc est corpus Christi" ("This is the body of Christ"). Wine was also blessed in the name of Jesus, but only the priests drank it. The Catholic Church taught that during Communion, Christ was truly present in the Host and the blessed wine.

Mass was celebrated every day, although weekday services were shorter and simpler than those on Sunday. In addition to Communion, hymns, prayers, and readings from the Bible were always part of Mass. Much of the service was sung or chanted, and nuns and churchmen often found great satisfaction in composing beautiful music for this most important religious celebration.

In addition to Mass, there were eight other services, known together as the Divine Office. These were ceremonies of prayer and praise. Each service in the Divine Office included hymns, Bible verses, prayers, and from three to nine psalms (poems from the Book of Psalms in the Bible). In medieval monasteries and cathedrals, every word of these services was sung.

The Divine Office began with matins, which was sung a little after midnight or around 2:00 a.m. Lauds was held at dawn or even earlier. Prime, terce, sext, and none were roughly three hours apart, from about 6:00 a.m. to about 3:00 p.m. In the evening, vespers was celebrated. The final service before bed was compline. The Franciscans made this a special, longer service and encouraged ordinary people to attend it at the end of their workday. Church bells rang to signal the beginning of each service, and also marking the passage of time.

Daily Monastery Life

Monastery life revolved around the routine of Mass and the Divine Office. The entire community attended Mass twice each day. After the morning service, monks or nuns wound their way through the cloister to their chapter house. Here they listened to a chapter of the rule being read aloud (this activity gave the building its name) and discussed monastery business and spiritual matters. Sometimes the abbot or a senior monk gave a lecture. This was also a time for everyone to examine their own conduct and one another's. If anyone's behavior was found faulty, the abbot or prior would discipline them.

After sext, around noon, the monks or nuns went to the lavatorium to wash their hands, which was often done with great ceremony. Then they went into the refectory for their first meal of the day. In summertime, they were allowed to take a nap or read after this meal. They would have another meal in the evening, before vespers. In winter, however, they were supposed to have only one meal a day, in the middle of the afternoon. At every meal, one of the monks or nuns read aloud from a religious book. Everyone else listened and ate in total silence. If they needed to communicate, they used sign language. For example, if a monk made a circle with the thumbs and forefingers of both his hands, it meant, "Please pass the bread."

The Rule of Saint Benedict instructed, "Idleness is the enemy of the soul; and therefore the brethren ought to be employed in manual labor at certain times, at others, in devout reading." Ideally, monks and nuns spent time every morning working and time every afternoon reading. The work could take many forms, including the cleaning and upkeep of the monastery, tending the community's beehives or gardens, making candlesticks or clothes, and copying out or illustrating books. When it was time for study, monks and nuns chose their reading from works of philosophy, religious thought, history, and ancient literature. On Sundays, they were not supposed to work, unless they had assigned tasks such as serving the meals, but to spend all their free hours reading.

As time went on, monks and nuns did less actual work, unless they belonged to a very small or poor monastery. Church services were getting longer and more elaborate. In many places, services took up almost every moment of the monks' or nuns' day, so that there was only time left for eating and sleeping. However, worship and prayer were felt to be the true work of the monasteries. The work of lay brothers and sisters allowed monks and nuns the freedom to follow this calling.

Chapter Eight

A Year of Religious Observances

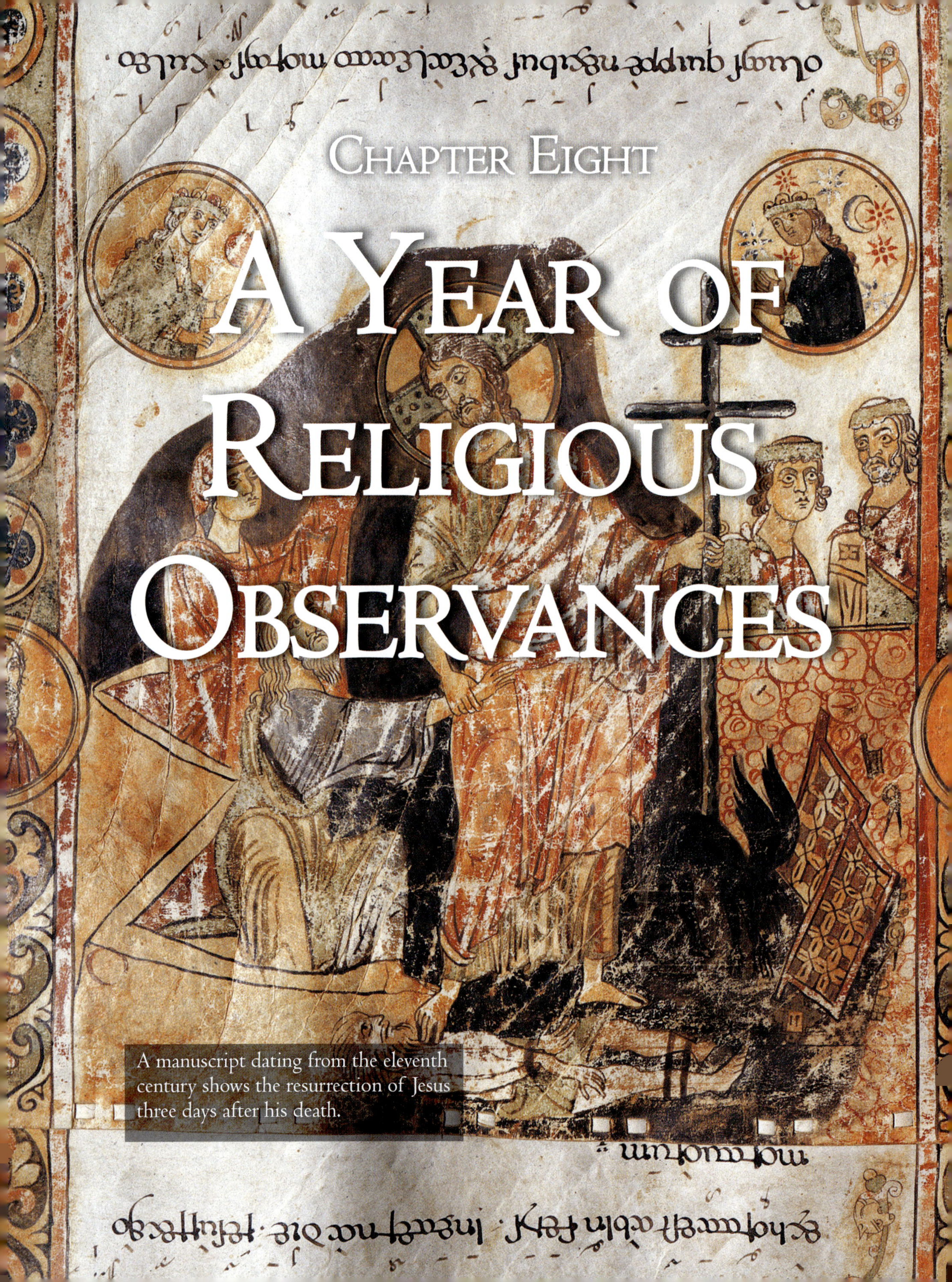

A manuscript dating from the eleventh century shows the resurrection of Jesus three days after his death.

"Jesus said unto her, I am the resurrection, and the life: he that believeth in me, though he were dead, yet shall he live: And whosoever liveth and believeth in me shall never die. Believest thou this?

—John 11:25–26

The medieval year was marked by religious observances. In monasteries, the seasons dictated the daily activities of monks and nuns. For all members of medieval society, the calendar year was broken up by religious celebrations, including the Christmas and Easter seasons and dozens of feast days in honor of the saints.

In the summer, monks and nuns took advantage of the longer hours of daylight to read and study. Because of the lengthy day they were allowed two meals; because of the heat, they did less work. In winter, with its shorter days, monastery residents ate only one meal. They read less and did more work than in the summer—but they also got more sleep during the long hours of darkness. The passing of the year was also marked by many holy days. In fact, nearly every day of the calendar was dedicated to a saint or to the memory of an event in the life of Jesus or the Virgin Mary. Parts of Mass and of the Divine Office changed day by day to mark these observances.

Throughout Christendom, the greatest holy days were Christmas and Easter. These important days might be the only times all year that nuns and monks took baths. Christmas marked the birth of Jesus. Before Christmas, there was a season of preparation called Advent. When Christmas finally arrived, it was celebrated with three Masses, the first one being held at midnight. In the medieval church, Christmas Day was a joyous but solemn holiday.

During the Christmas season, however, some not-so-serious customs were observed in many churches and monasteries. For example, on the Feast of Saint Nicholas (December 6), a "boy bishop" was chosen from among the children of the monastery school, grammar school, or cathedral choir. This boy was dressed up in elaborate robes and led a procession around the parish, giving his blessing to the people. Similarly, in some women's monasteries a young girl acted as abbess for a limited time.

The boy bishop, sitting on the bishop's throne in the cathedral, might also be part of the Feast of Fools, celebrated on or around January 1. During the Divine Office on this day, clergy members sometimes wore masks or dressed up as women or had their clothes on inside out. They held their service books upside down and sang out-of-tune nonsense syllables. Instead of making their way around the church with dignity, they ran and leaped about. During Mass, they munched on sausages and heehawed like donkeys at the end of the service—and the congregation heehawed in response. Church authorities strongly disapproved of these customs, but they were popular throughout Europe, especially France.

Very soon it was time to get serious again. The Christmas season ended on January 6 with the Feast of Epiphany. On this day, church services recalled three important events in the life of Jesus: the wise men kneeling to honor him, his baptism, and his first miracle.

Devout followers paved the streets of Jerusalem with palm fronds as Jesus rode in atop a donkey.

Liturgical Drama

In Chester, England, townspeople gather in the central square to watch a play based on Jesus's life and teachings.

Beginning in the tenth century, liturgical dramas were plays staged in the church that enacted holy scenes. These plays were performed in Latin and made use of props, costumes, and sets. The earliest known liturgical drama was the *Quem quaeritis*, which translates from Latin as "Whom do you seek?" It reenacted the visit to Jesus's tomb after his crucifixion.

Popular stories depicted scenes from the life of Jesus, such as his birth and resurrection, as well as events in the lives of holy saints. These plays were used to educate the masses on the teachings of Christianity. During the spring and summer months, plays were often staged outdoors. By the 1500s, medieval drama had become more secular and was no longer reserved for holy productions.

In February or March, Lent began. Lent, the forty days before Easter, was a time when people were expected to be mindful of their sins and to try to put themselves right with God. Monks and nuns were supposed to have only one meal a day during Lent. The Rule of Saint Benedict taught, "The life of a monk ought always to be a Lenten observance … We advise that during these days of Lent he guard his life with all purity and at the same time wash away … all the shortcomings of other times ... During these days, therefore, let us add something to the usual amount of our service … let [each one] withdraw from his body somewhat of food, drink, sleep, speech, merriment, and with the gladness of spiritual desire await holy Easter."

Toward the end of Lent came Palm Sunday, the beginning of Holy Week. Palm Sunday celebrated the arrival of Jesus in Jerusalem, when people paved his way with palm branches. In the Middle Ages, priests blessed palm, olive, or willow branches. They then distributed the branches among worshipers, who carried them in a procession before Mass, singing joyful hymns. A large carved wooden figure of Jesus riding a donkey was often pulled along in this procession.

The Thursday of Holy Week remembered Jesus's Last Supper. Before the meal, Jesus had washed the feet of all his disciples. In the Middle Ages, poor people, the elderly, and children were invited to monasteries to have their feet washed and receive gifts of food and money. At Westminster Abbey in London, the abbot himself washed the feet of thirteen elderly men, while the monks washed the feet of children.

The next day, Good Friday, was a solemn day of mourning, for it commemorated the death of Jesus. On Saturday night, monks, nuns, and secular clergymen decorated their churches. All of the bright, beautiful candlesticks, crosses, and other ornaments of the church had been covered or put away for Lent. Now they were brought out again, ready for the dawning of Easter morning. With as many as five hundred candles lighting the church, the celebration of the most holy day of the year began. At Easter, Christians remembered the resurrection of Jesus and his promise of eternal life.

Chapter Nine

Corruption and Heresy

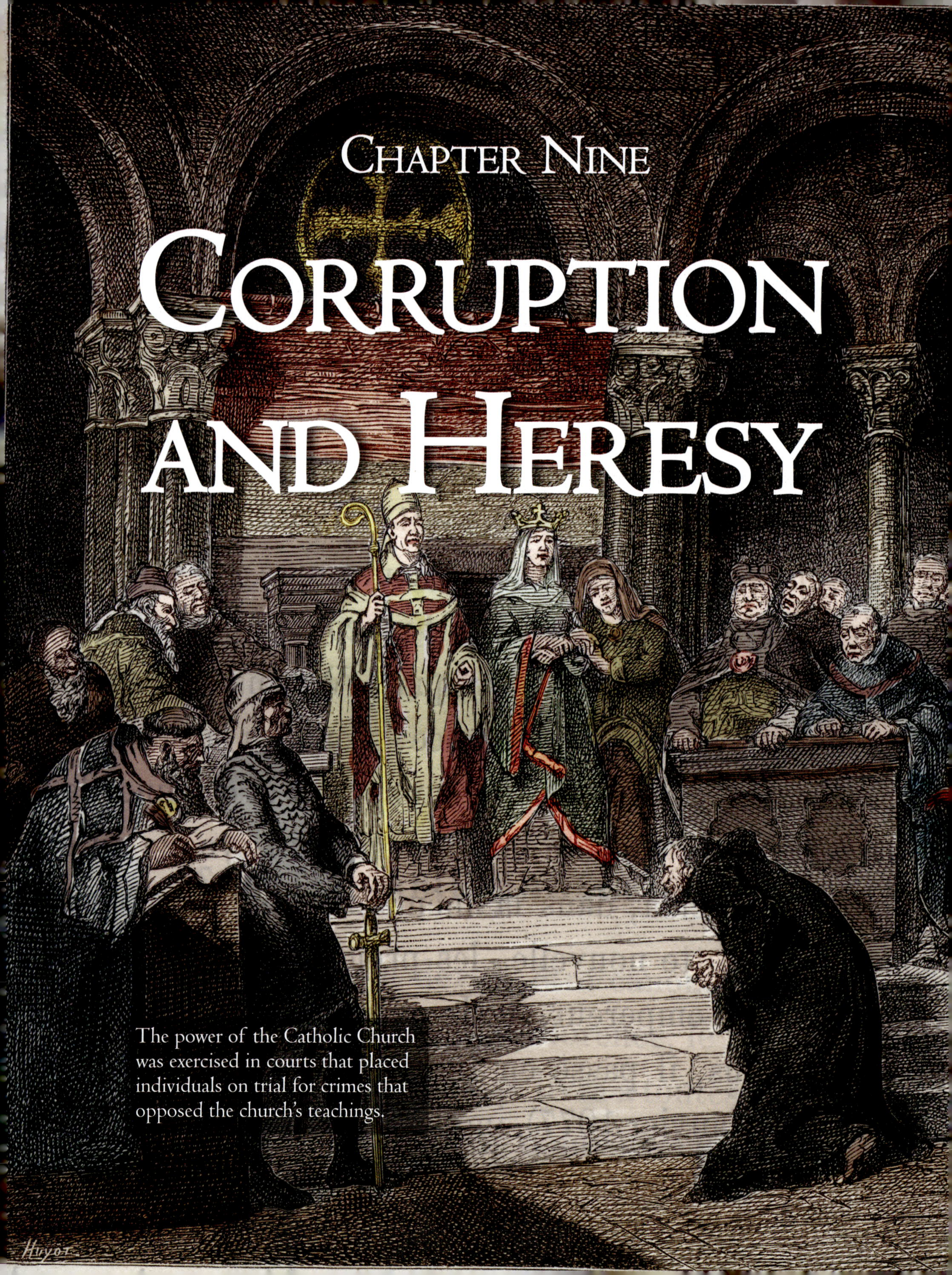

The power of the Catholic Church was exercised in courts that placed individuals on trial for crimes that opposed the church's teachings.

“I see the pope his sacred trust betray,
For while the rich his grace can gain alway,
His favors from the poor are aye withholden.
He strives to gather wealth as best he may,
Forcing Christ’s people blindly to obey,
So that he may repose in garments golden.”
—Rainon de Cornet, a fourteenth-century troubadour, on the corruption of the pope as the head of the Catholic Church

By the High Middle Ages, the Catholic Church was a powerful force, inextricably linked to the state. Not all people were content to live under the authority of the Christian religion. The church often turned to corruption and violence to retain its power over medieval Europeans.

Nuns and churchmen of the Middle Ages were expected to live according to very high standards. They did not always succeed, for they were prone to the same human failings as everyone else. Nevertheless, they were often criticized for not living up to the church’s ideals. They were charged with being greedy, lazy, selfish, corrupt, stupid, and worse.

Sometimes the criticism was deserved. There were many country priests who did not understand the Latin words they spoke during Mass. There were many bishops who never visited their dioceses and who were more involved in politics than in religion. There were nuns who entertained guests in luxurious rooms at their monasteries and monks who ate till they were fat and drank till they were drunk. There were popes who sided with one European government against another and used their powers for their own personal ends. These situations were worse at some times than at others. Usually the periods of great corruption were followed by periods of great reform.

Throughout the High Middle Ages in western Europe, there seems to have been a large number of people sincerely seeking a deep and personal experience of religion. Sometimes these people did not find what they were looking for in the established Catholic Church. Instead, they turned to religious movements that frequently went against official Christian teachings. The Catholic Church called these movements **heresies**.

The most powerful heresy of the Middle Ages was Catharism, which flourished especially in southern France. Cathars taught that humans were a mixture of spirit and matter; spirit was created by a good God, and matter and all evils were created by an evil God. It was possible, the Cathars believed, to rise above matter and evil to reach spiritual perfection in this life. Although the Cathars were still Christians, they also taught that Jesus had never really become human. They believed that even in his time on earth he had been completely spiritual. In addition, the Cathars allowed women to play an equal role with men in religion.

Even though most Cathars lived quiet, decent, family-centered lives, the Catholic Church found their ideas very dangerous. In the early thirteenth century, the pope sent out many preachers to try to bring the Cathars back to the Catholicism's teachings. When this did not work, the pope allowed the nobles of northern France to mount a crusade against southern France.

On Pilgrimage to Canterbury

Geoffrey Chaucer, who lived from about 1340 to 1400, was one of the greatest writers in English literature. His most famous book is *The Canterbury Tales*, in which a group of people on a pilgrimage to the shrine of Saint Thomas à Becket in Canterbury entertain one another by telling stories. Among the pilgrims are a prioress, a monk, and a friar. None of them appear to be living entirely according to the ideals of religious orders. At the time Chaucer was writing, many people were very critical of monastic life and felt that most monks and nuns were too worldly. Chaucer seems to have agreed. Here, in a modern English adaptation, is his portrait of the friar.

THE FRIAR

There was a friar, who was merry and wild …
He was friendly and very well loved
By wealthy landowners all around
And by worthy women of the town …
He very nicely heard confession;
And so that he would get a good donation,
He went easy when he gave penance;
His absolution was not unpleasant …
For many a man is so hard of heart,
That he will not weep although he is hurt;
Therefore, instead of weeping and saying prayers,
Men often give silver to the poor friars.
This friar's hood was always filled with knives
And pins and other gifts for fair housewives.

And certainly he had a merry voice
As he sang and played his instrument of choice …
He was as strong as a champion.

He knew the taverns well in every town,
And knew every barmaid and innkeeper
Better than he knew any beggar or leper.
For to such a worthy man as he,
By his way of thinking, it was unseemly
To have any acquaintance with the lowly poor;
It was not respectable and it got him nowhere
To deal with outcasts and the rabble,
Instead of with the rich and sellers of victuals!
And with everyone from whom he could get money
He was as courteous and humble as could be.
There was no other man so virtuous;
He was the best beggar of his house.

This was the first major outbreak of violent intolerance between different groups of European Christians. It was not the last, and it was echoed by new waves of prejudice and violence against Jews, Muslims, and other non-Christians. The church formed a new office, the Inquisition, dedicated to rooting out heresy and making sure that people followed only accepted teachings.

On the heels of religious conflict, as the Middle Ages drew to a close, the church began to lose hold of its power. The common people began to turn away from the authority of the church. People continued to seek out personal relationships with God and embody the good and righteous lessons taught by Jesus.

The Inquisition

Heretics are burned at the stake by the order of King Phillip II of France in this illumination from 1210.

As the Catholic Church began to meet with opposition across Europe, inquisitors were sent out to bring the masses back under its control. People guilty of heresy were given thirty days to profess their sins against the church. For those who did not repent, trials were held. It was common for the accused to be tortured to obtain confessions. After the trials, the guilty were sentenced at a public ceremony called the *sermo generalis*. For those who repented, common punishments included forced pilgrimages and prison sentences, as well as being publicly labeled and ostracized by wearing yellow crosses. For those who would not repent, their punishment was death, usually by burning at the stake.

Some kings and queens did not support the Inquisition, while others embraced it. In Spain, under the rule of King Ferdinand and Queen Isabella, the Inquisition was an especially bloody time. Over 200,000 people were burned at the stake, and more than 160,000 Jews were forced out of Spain. In some areas, the Inquisition lasted for approximately seven hundred years.

Glossary

abbey

A monastery headed by an abbot, the highest rank of monk; an abbey could have a number of other monasteries called priories under its authority.

altarpiece

A painting or carved panel at the back of the altar; it usually showed episodes from the lives of Jesus and the saints.

bishop

A high-ranking churchman who oversees religious affairs for a particular region.

brazier

A portable metal container for a small fire or hot coals.

cathedral

A church where a bishop has his headquarters; the word comes from *cathedra,* meaning "throne," because the bishop had his throne, symbolizing his authority, behind the high altar of this church.

chapter house

The building where monks or nuns gathered every day to hear the reading of a chapter of their rule and to conduct monastery business.

cloister

A square or rectangular covered walkway around a garden or open area.

disciple

A devoted student or follower.

double monastery

A monastery for both men and women, where they lived in separate, neighboring buildings and were both ruled by one superior.

dowry

Money or property that a woman brings into marriage.

friar

A monk belonging to the Franciscan or Dominican order; the word comes from the Latin *frater*, meaning "brother."

heresy

A belief or viewpoint that is in opposition to the teachings of a particular religion or institution.

homage

Actions or words that express special honor and respect.

humanist

Someone adhering to a belief system based on a basic belief in goodness in people and that problems can be solved through rational reasoning, as opposed to religious faith.

Islam

The religion founded by Muhammad in seventh-century Arabia; Islam means "submission to God."

knight

A warrior of the noble class, trained to fight on horseback.

lay brother or sister

A man or woman who took the vows of poverty, chastity, and obedience and lived in a monastery but did the everyday work of the monastery instead of taking part in all the daily religious services.

missionary

A person who travels to a far-off place to teach his or her religion to the people of that place.

monastery

A community of men or women who devoted themselves to prayer, study, and work; also, the buildings that house such a community

monotheistic

The belief in a single, all-powerful god.

Muslim

A follower of the religion of Islam.

nave

The main part of a church, where the people gathered to attend religious services.

parchment

Sheepskin or goatskin specially prepared for writing on.

penance

Actions undertaken to show sorrow for and make up for sinful behavior.

pilgrimage

A journey to an important religious site; for example, a church that housed the remains of a saint.

refectory

The monastery building where monks and nuns had their meals.

relic

Part of a deceased holy person's body or possessions kept as an object of deep respect.

rule

A book that gave guidance and rules for monastery life.

saint

A person recognized by the Catholic Church as being especially holy and able to perform miracles both during life and after death.

secular

"In the world," moving among ordinary people and taking part in everyday life.

superior

The abbot, abbess, prior, or prioress who was the head of a monastery.

tonsure

A haircut that left the top of the head bald.

Further Information

Books

Kallen, Stuart A. *Life During the Crusades*. San Diego, CA: ReferencePoint Press, 2014.

Logan, F. Donald. *A History of the Church in the Middle Ages*. New York: Routledge, 2012.

Macaulay, David. *Cathedral*. New York: HMH Books for Young Readers, 2013.

McAleavy, Tony. *Life in a Medieval Abbey*. New York: Enchanted Lion Books, 2010.

Rosewell, Roger. *The Medieval Monastery*. Oxford, UK: Shire, 2012.

Websites

Church in the Middle Ages: From Dedication to Dissent
www.bl.uk/the-middle-ages/articles/church-in-the-middle-ages-frrom-dedication-to-dissent
Read about the Catholic Church's rise to power in the Middle Ages in this article by the British Library.

Fragmented Devotion
www.bc.edu/bc_org/avp/cas/artmuseum/exhibitions/archive/fragment/church.html
Take a virtual tour of religious artifacts from the medieval era through the Schnütgen Museum in Cologne, Germany.

Life in a Monastery
www.oblatespring.com/Resources/Feltonfleet%20School%20Monastic%20life.pdf
Learn about life in a medieval monastery.

Films

Building the Great Cathedrals. NOVA, 2010.

The Crusades: Crescent and The Cross. The History Channel, 2005.

Organizations

Canadian Society of Medievalists
www.canadianmedievalists.ca/index.php?lang=en
The Canadian Society of Medievalists is an organization dedicated to medieval studies. The society publishes an annual journal, *Florilegium*, and hosts an annual conference for medieval enthusiasts.

The Medieval Academy of America
www.medievalacademy.org
As the largest medieval organization in the United States, the Medieval Academy of America focuses on all areas of life during the Middle Ages. The academy holds annual conferences, publishes research, and offers a student membership.

Source Notes

Ch. 1: The Rise of Christianity

p. 7, "The Capitulary of Charlemagne," retrieved from https://legacy.fordham.edu/halsall/basis/einhard.asp.

Ch. 2: A Christian Europe

p. 13, biblical verses retrieved from https://www.kingjamesbibleonline.org/1-John-5-7.

p. 16, Scott-Stokes, Charity. *Women's Books of Hours in Medieval England.* Suffolk, UK: D.S. Brewer, 2012. p. 94.

Ch. 3: The Church Community

p. 19, French, Katherine L. *The People of the Parish: Community Life in a Late Medieval English Diocese.* Philadelphia: University of Pennsylvania Press, 2012. p. 1.

Ch. 4: A Pious Life

p. 27, *The Order of St. Benedict*, retrieved from http://www.osb.org/rb/text/rbejms3.html#7.

Ch. 5: Medieval Nuns

p. 37, quote by Hildegard of Bingen, retrieved from http://web.clark.edu/afisher/HIST252/lectures_text/women_religious_roles_middleages.pdf.

p. 40, Hagopian, Landon. *The Esoteric Codex: Christian Mysticism.* Lulu.com. p. 179.

Ch. 6: A Religious Childhood

p. 47, quote by William of Canterbury, retrieved from http://www.ncbi.nlm.nih.gov/pmc/articles/PMC1036334/pdf/medhist00051-0003.pdf.

Ch. 7: Labors in the Name of the Lord

p. 53, quote by Ælfric of Eynsham retrieved from http://www.medievalists.net/2016/01/31/those-who-pray-those-who-work-those-who-fight.

Ch. 8: A Year of Religious Celebrations

p. 57, biblical verses retrieved from https://www.kingjamesbibleonline.org/John-Chapter-11.

Ch. 9: Corruption and Heresy

p. 63, "Raimon de Cornet: Poem Criticizing the Avignon Papacy," retrieved from http://legacy.fordham.edu/Halsall/source/14Ccornet.asp.

p. 65–66, Chauer, Geoffrey. *The Canterbury Tales: A Selection*. Edited by Donald R. Howard. New York: New American Library, 1969. Excerpts adapted by Kathryn Hinds.

Bibliography

Armstrong, Regis J., and Ignatius C. Brady, trans. *Francis and Clare: The Complete Works*. New York: Paulist Press, 1982.

Banks, Mary Maclead, ed. "Alphabet of Tales" in *Corpus of Middle English Prose and Verse*. http://www.hti.umich.edu/english/mideng.

Blanchard, Laura V., and Carolyn Schriber. "ORB: The Online Reference Book for Medieval Studies." http://orb.rhodes.edu.

Brooke, Christopher. *The Monastic World 1000–1300*. New York: Random House, 1974.

Burr, David, trans. *Thomas of Celano's First and Second Lives of Saint Francis*. http://dburr.hist.vt.edu/Celano.html.

Burton, Janet. *Monastic and Religious Orders in Britain 1000–1300*. New York: Cambridge University Press, 1994.

Cantor, Norman F. *The Civilization of the Middle Ages*. New York: Harper Perennial, 1994.

Catholic Encyclopedia, The. http://www.newadvent.org/cathen.

Chaucer, Geoffrey. *The Canterbury Tales: A Selection*. Edited by Donald R. Howard. New York: New American Library, 1969.

DeGregorio, Scott. "Guide to On-line Resources in Medieval Spirituality." http://www.chass.utoronto.ca/~degregor/spirituality.html.

De Hamel, Christopher. *Medieval Craftsmen: Scribes and Illuminators*. Toronto: University of Toronto Press, 1992.

Editors of Time-Life Books. *What Life Was Like in the Age of Chivalry: Medieval Europe a.d. 800–1500*. Alexandria, VA: Time-Life Books, 1997.

Gies, Frances, and Joseph Gies. *Cathedral, Forge, and Waterwheel: Technology and Invention in the Middle Ages*. New York: HarperCollins, 1994.

———. *Women in the Middle Ages*. New York: Barnes & Noble, 1978.

Hallam, Elizabeth, ed. *Chronicles of the Crusades: Nine Crusades and Two Hundred Years of Bitter Conflict for the Holy Land Brought to Life through the Words of Those Who Were Actually There*. New York: Weidenfeld and Nicolson, 1989.

Halsall, Paul, ed. "Internet Medieval Sourcebook." http://www.fordham.edu/halsall/sbook.html.

Harbin, Beau A. C. "NetSERF: The Internet Connection for Medieval Resources." http://netserf.cua.edu.

Hoppin, Richard H. *Medieval Music*. New York: Norton, 1978.

Irvine, Martin, and Deborah Everhart. "The Labyrinth: Resources for Medieval Studies." http://www.georgetown.edu/labyrinth.

Luria, Maxwell S., and Richard L. Hoffman, eds. *Middle English Lyrics*. New York: Norton, 1974.

Metford, J. C. J. *Dictionary of Christian Lore and Legend*. London: Thames and Hudson, 1983.

Riley-Smith, Jonathan, ed. *The Oxford Illustrated History of the Crusades*. Oxford, UK: Oxford University Press, 1995.

Shahar, Shulamith. *Childhood in the Middle Ages*. Trans;ated by Chaya Galai. New York: Routledge, 1990.

———. *The Fourth Estate: A History of Women in the Middle Ages*. Translated by Chaya Galai. New York: Methuen, 1983.

Verheyen, Boniface, OSB, trans. *The Holy Rule of Saint Benedict*. http://www.benedictine.edu/abbey/site1/framemn.htm.

Index

Page numbers in **boldface** are illustrations. Entries in **boldface** are glossary terms.